Intermediate to Advanced Piano Solo

THE WORLD'S GREAT CLASSICAL MUSIC

Beethoven

36 Selections from Symphonies, Concertos, Masses and Piano Works

EDITED BY BLAKE NEELY AND RICHARD WALTERS

D0899758

ISBN 0-634-02780-8

HAL•LEONARD®
CORPORATION
7777 W. BLUEMOUND RD. P.O. BOX 13819 MILWAUKEE, WI 53213

Visit Hal Leonard Online at
www.halleonard.com

CONTENTS

Pieces originally for solo piano; the remaining works are piano transcriptions.

LUDWIG VAN BEETHOVEN
1770-1827

Nearly two centuries after they were written, the opening bars of Beethoven's Symphony No. 5 still strike listeners as a powerful, distinctive musical statement. History recalls Beethoven as the great innovator who pointed music in the direction of the Romantic era, leaving the reserve and veneer of the Classical behind. In order to understand how stunning the Fifth Symphony was to the audience at its 1808 premiere, it is important to remember that the more discreet sounds of Mozart, C.P.E. Bach and Haydn were still quite popular. Haydn was still alive. Beethoven was only 14 years younger than Mozart, and was born just 20 years after J.S. Bach's death. Beethoven met Mozart at least once. He studied with Haydn and with Mozart's rival, Antonio Salieri. Yet he chose to toss aside the stylistic traits of his teachers in order to carve out a bold style of his own.

The ears of the public were not ready for the power and passion of Beethoven's music. The great poet Goethe, who admired Beethoven, after hearing the composer play the opening of Symphony No. 5 on the piano, commented that it sounded as if the whole house was about to come down. A Vienna critic wrote of the overture to *Fidelio*, "...never was anything as incoherent, shrill, chaotic and ear-splitting produced in music." Another Vienna critic referred to Symphony No. 2 as "...a crass monster, a hideously wounded dragon, that refuses to expire, and though bleeding in the finale, furiously beats about with its tail erect." John Ruskin wrote, "Beethoven always sounds to me like the upsetting of bags of nails with here and there an also dropped hammer."

Many things about the life and music of Beethoven were strikingly different from the model created for him by previous generations of musicians. He viewed himself as a great artist, one to whom the world owed a living. In contrast, Mozart, who justifiably regarded himself as a genius, never referred to himself as an artist. Musicians in Beethoven's day were largely beholden to nobility or to a church for employment. In neither case did they have much freedom to choose what to write or where they might work or travel. Although Beethoven had no problem accepting patronage from the wealthy nobility, he was never employed by them. In fact, he demanded to be treated as an equal by the nobles, and when one of his patrons stopped sending money, Beethoven confronted him, demanding that the payments resume.

Ludwig van Beethoven was born in December of 1770, the son of a professional musician in service to the court at Bonn. He acquired various training there in keyboard playing, violin and composition, combined with valuable experiences playing in ensembles and as a soloist. Several important friendships were formed in Bonn. In his youth, Ludwig was socially quite active, and many of his early compositions were written for musical evenings with society friends. His great friend Count Waldstein was the one who suggested Beethoven should move to Vienna to study composition with Haydn, writing in a letter, "With the help of assiduous labor you shall receive Mozart's spirit from Haydn's hands." The pupil-teacher relationship between Beethoven and Haydn was not a particularly happy one, and was fairly short-lived. However, it did get Ludwig to Vienna in 1792, where he would live the rest of his life.

Beethoven's strength of personality was evident in every aspect of his life. As a pianist, which is how he first captured the public's attention, he was a bold, powerful performer. He was known for striking the piano with such force that he routinely broke strings. He frequently pleaded with piano manufacturers of the time to make a louder instrument that was more able to withstand his demands. Whether these demands were the result of early stages of his now famous deafness may never be known.

Beethoven was not an attractive man. He was short, with a head too large for his body. His skin was ruddy, mottled and pockmarked, his hair wild and bushy. He was short tempered, a trait that only increased as his hearing failed. He was a difficult tenant, moving frequently to new lodgings after alienating one landlord after another. His quarters were notoriously sloppy, and he treated his domestic help so poorly that they were continually fleeing to find a less taxing employer. He was also a difficult student, making a mockery of such rules as the forbidding of parallel fifths.

Although his relationships with women were not much more successful, there were a few women in his life. He dedicated some of his piano pieces to these women, including his Sonata No. 14 ("Moonlight") to Countess Giulietta Guicciardi. One of these women remains a great mystery. A letter found in his belongings after his death is addressed to "My Immortal Beloved." He refers to her as "my angel, my all, my very self." He states, "our love is truly founded in heaven." He begs her to "continue to love me, never misjudge your lover's most faithful heart." Although scholars have long searched for the identity of the woman to whom this ardent letter was written, she remains an intriguing mystery.

He did little better with family relationships. In 1815 his brother Caspar Karl died leaving a wife and son. In his will Casper Karl named his wife Johanna and his brother Ludwig to serve as joint guardians for his son Karl. He noted in the will that "the best of harmony" did not exist between Johanna and Ludwig and stressed that he did not want his son to be taken away from his mother. But Ludwig decided that Johanna was not fit to raise the boy and began a long, ugly custody battle. He eventually won and placed the boy in a boarding school. Johanna appealed a few years later and began another court battle, which unearthed some messy history about Beethoven's family. It seems that Beethoven's father had falsified the family's status as minor nobility some years earlier, adding the "van" to the name. When this story came out, the court battle was bumped down to commoner's court. Beethoven won again, but at great personal cost. He produced little music during these years. In 1826, the twenty-year-old Karl attempted suicide, later referring to "imprisonment" in Beethoven's home. The suicide attempt left his uncle "looking like a man of seventy years," according to some of his friends.

As painful as the saga of his nephew was to him, the greatest tragedy of Beethoven's life was the loss of his most precious sense, his hearing. From about 1800 it became apparent that the composer's hearing was fading. Doctors could not help. While vacationing in Heiligenstadt in 1802, he wrote a letter to his brothers, which remained with his papers and was found after his death. He wrote, "Oh you who think or say that I am malevolent, stubborn or misanthropic, how greatly do you wrong me. You do not know the secret cause which makes me seem that way to you ... how could I possibly admit an infirmity in the one sense which ought to be more perfect in me than in others, a sense which I once enjoyed in the highest perfection..." Some believe that this letter is an indication of his thoughts of suicide. The onset of deafness greatly altered Ludwig's personality, which was previously highly social and boisterous. He became more and more reclusive. Yet Beethoven continued to work even after his deafness became complete from otosclerosis about 1817. He would converse with others by writing in notebooks, many of which have been preserved.

In the midst of his despair over his failing hearing, Beethoven wrote his Symphony No. 3, known as the "Eroica," (Heroic). It was with this piece that Beethoven departed stylistically from the Classical era. Though dedicated to Napoleon, when Bonaparte declared himself emperor, Beethoven destroyed the dedication in disgust, but continued working on the piece. The symphony, which premiered in 1805, was longer, more musically intense, and more difficult to play than anything that had been written to that point. Critics and audiences were divided, some calling it "bizarre," or writing that "it loses itself in lawlessness." To others it was a masterpiece.

Most of Beethoven's works were met with such divided responses. During rehearsals for the 1824 premiere of the Symphony No. 9, singers begged for the parts to be made more singable. Beethoven refused and the singers simply omitted the bits they could not sing. At the premiere of the symphony Beethoven had to be turned to face the audience so that he could see the applause that he could not hear. He had long been totally deaf as he wrote the Ninth, the Missa Solemnis, as well as several string quartets and piano sonatas.

Beethoven's failing health was destroyed in 1827 when he contracted pneumonia. He died in Vienna on March 23. The story is told that during a violent, snowy thunderstorm he opened his eyes, raised his right hand in a fist and then slumped back, dead. Whether or not that those details are true, it is known that between 20,000 and 30,000 people joined in his funeral procession through the streets of Vienna. The music that he left, much of which was revolutionary in its day, remains at the center of the world's concert literature to this day.

Elaine Schmidt

Agnus Dei
from Mass in D Major, "Missa Solemnis"

Ludwig van Beethoven
1770-1827
Op. 123
originally for soloists, chorus, organ and orchestra

Adagio

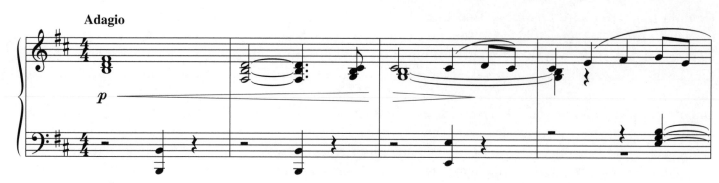

The Creatures of Prometheus
Overture Theme

Ludwig van Beethoven
1770-1827
Op. 43
originally for orchestra

10

Allegro molto con brio

Bagatelle in G Major

Ludwig van Beethoven
1770-1827
Op. 126, No. 5

The Consecration of the House Overture

Excerpt

Ludwig van Beethoven
1770-1827
Op. 124
originally for orchestra

Maestoso e sostenuto

19

Egmont Overture
Main Theme

Ludwig van Beethoven
1770-1827
Op. 84
originally for orchestra

Gloria
from Mass in C Major

Ludwig van Beethoven
1770-1827
Op. 86
originally for soloists, chorus, organ and orchestra

Allegro con brio

Leonore Overture No. 3

from the opera FIDELIO
Opening Theme

Ludwig van Beethoven
1770-1827
Op. 72
originally for orchestra

Rondo in C Major

Ludwig van Beethoven
1770–1827
Op. 51, No. 1

Moderato e grazioso

Piano Concerto No. 3 in C Minor

First Movement Excerpt

Ludwig van Beethoven
1770-1827
Op. 37
originally for piano and orchestra

Piano Concerto No. 5 in E-flat Major

"Emperor"
First Movement Excerpt

Ludwig van Beethoven
1770-1827
Op. 73
originally for piano and orchestra

Allegro

Rondo a capriccio in G Major
("Rage Over a Lost Penny")

Ludwig van Beethoven
1770–1827
Op. 129

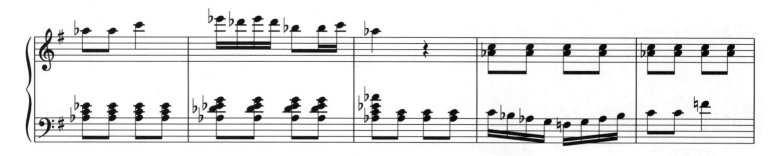

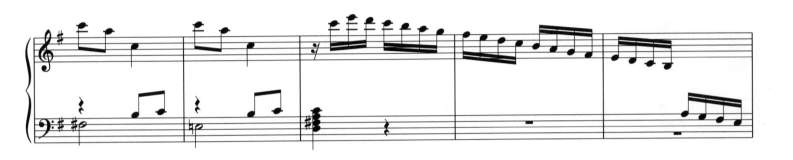

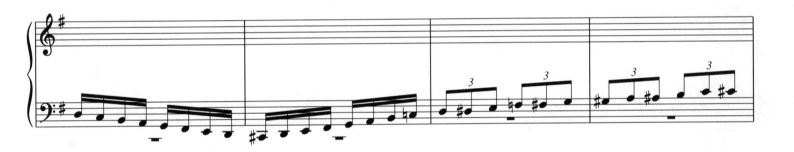

Rondo in G Major

Ludwig van Beethoven
1770–1827
Op. 51, No. 2

Andante cantabile e grazioso

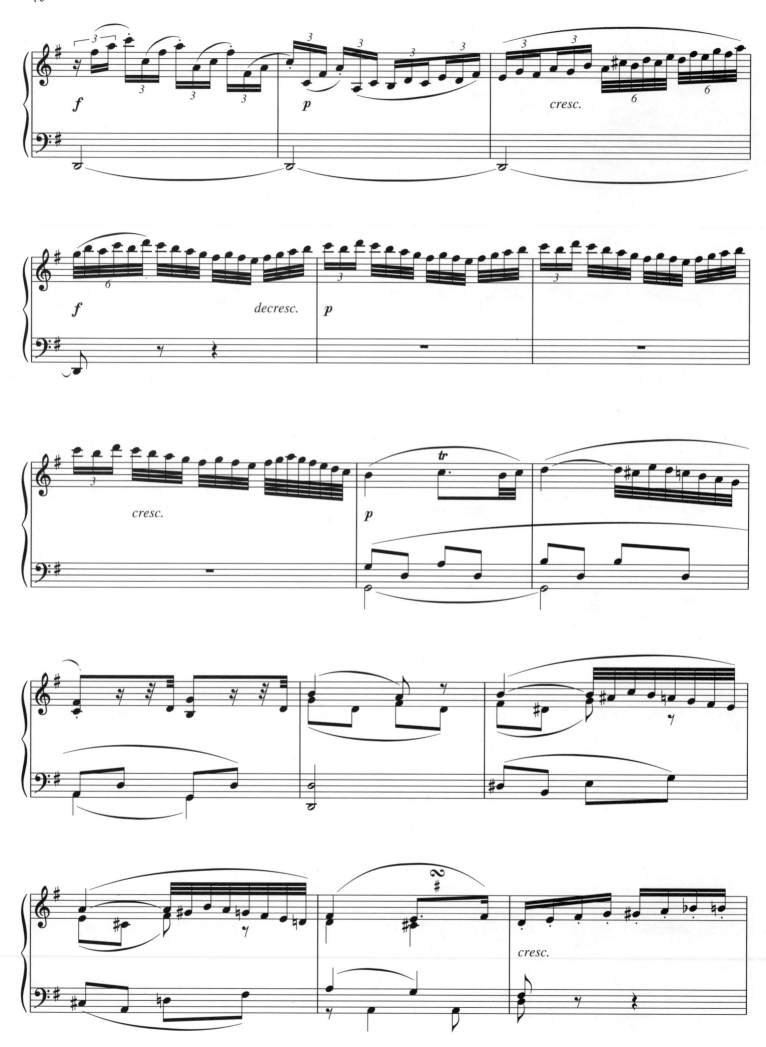

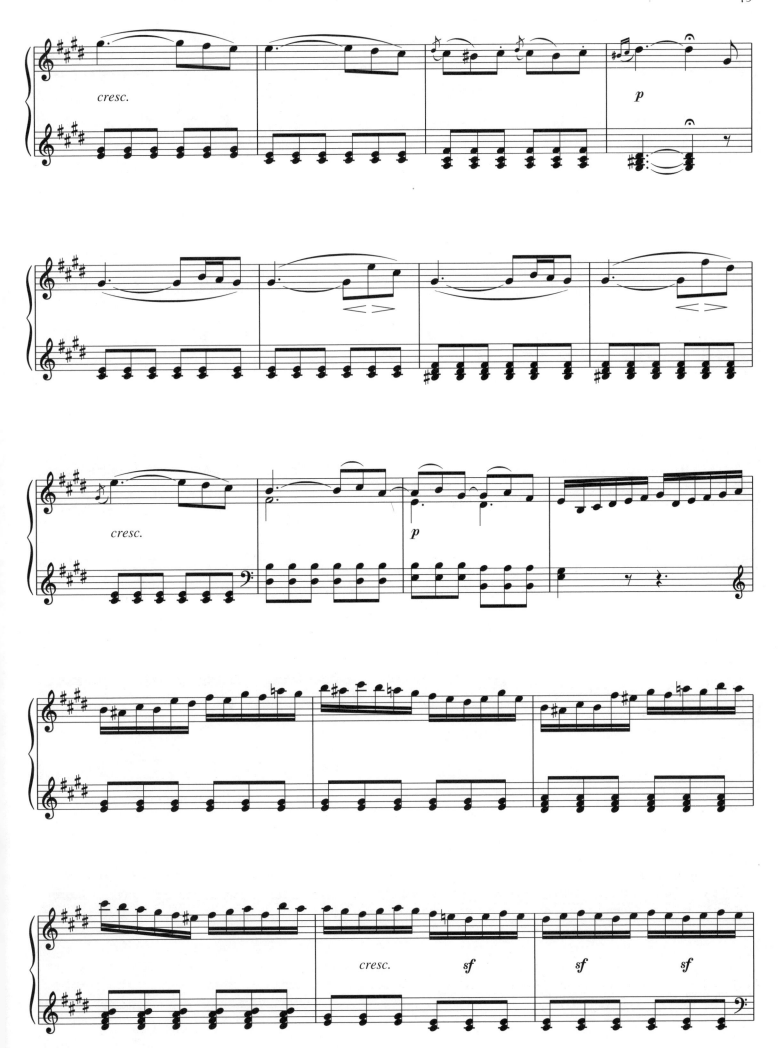

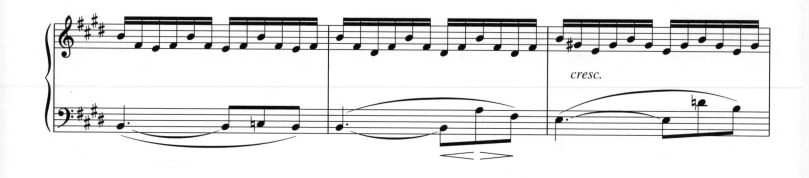

Sonata in C Minor
("Pathétique")

Ludwig van Beethoven
1770–1827
Op. 13

Allegro molto e con brio

88

Allegro molto e con brio

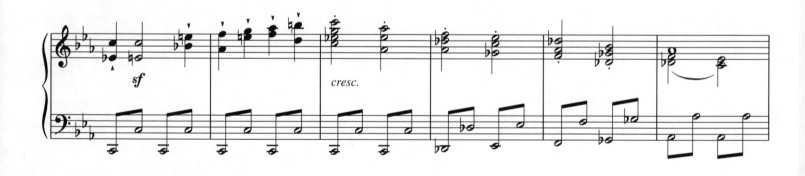

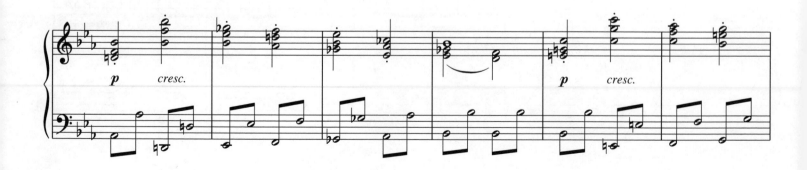

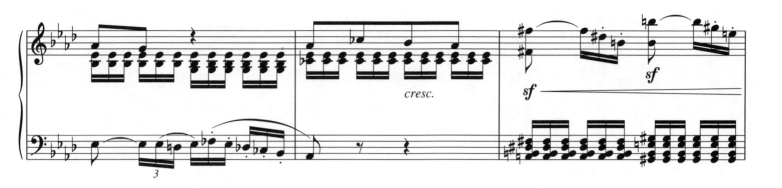

Rondo

Sonata in C-sharp Minor
("Moonlight")
First Movement

Ludwig van Beethoven
1770-1827
Op. 27, No. 2

Adagio sostenuto

Si deve suonare tutto questo pezzo delicatissimamente e senza sordino.

sempre **pp** *e senza sordino*

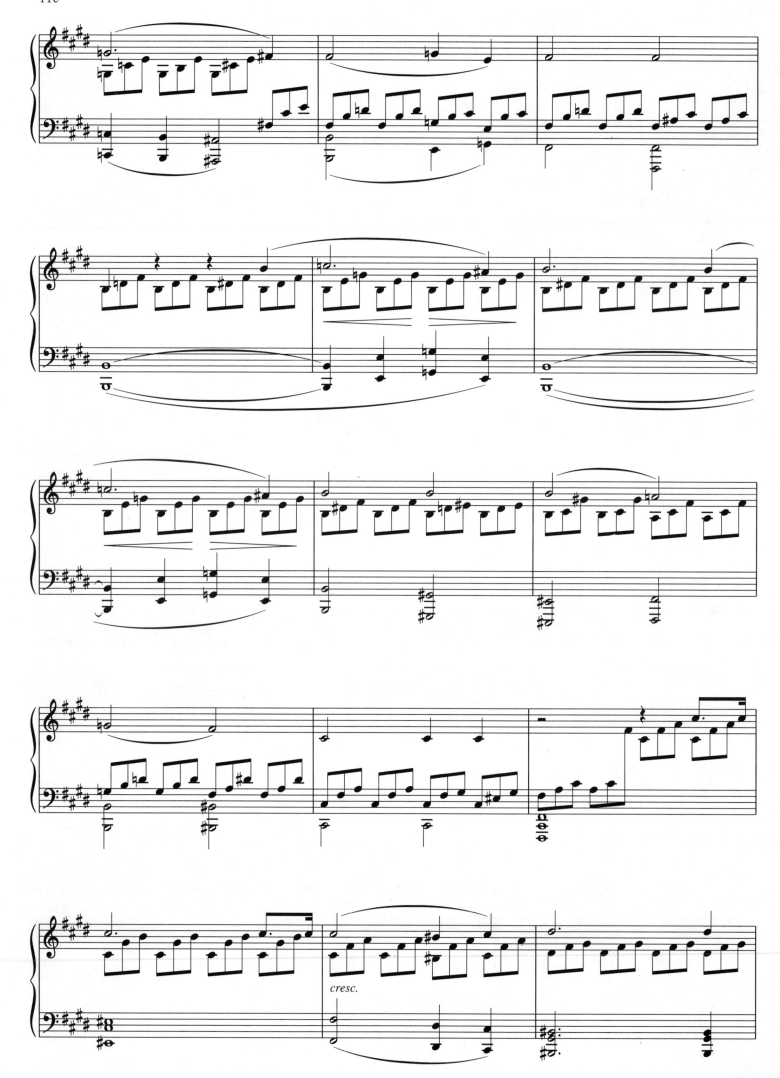

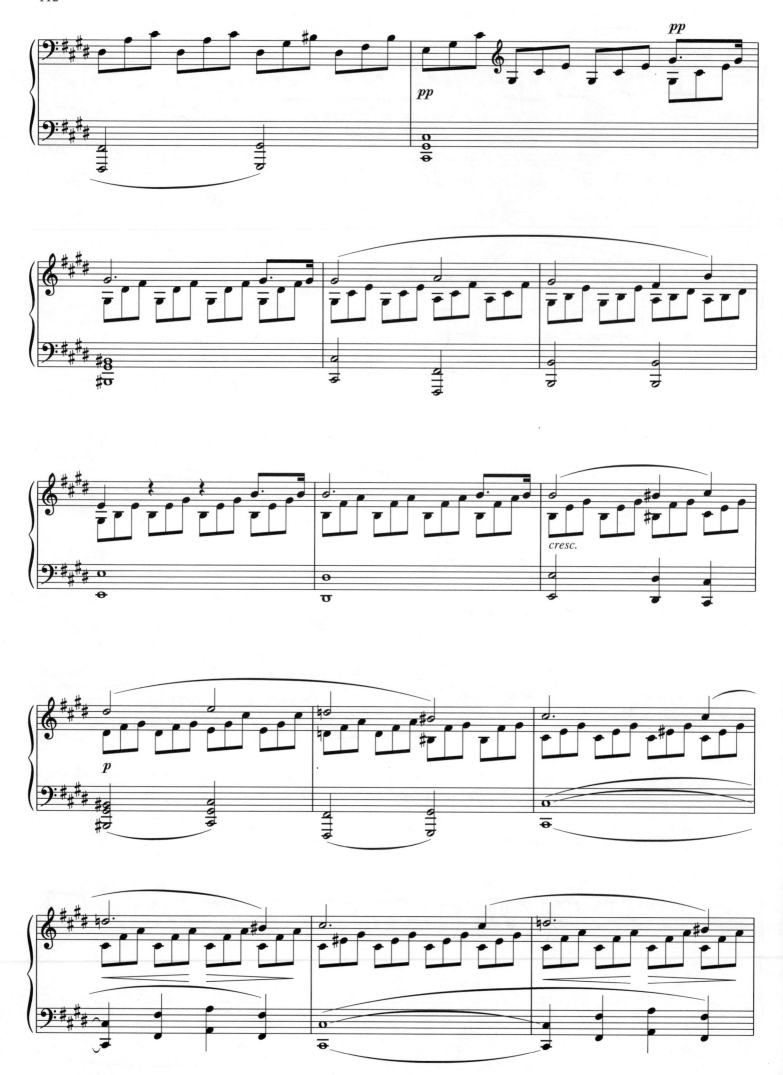

Symphony No. 1 in C Major

First Movement Excerpt

Ludwig van Beethoven
1770-1827
Op. 21
originally for orchestra

Symphony No. 1 in C Major

Third Movement Excerpt, "Minuet"

Ludwig van Beethoven
1770-1827
Op. 21
originally for orchestra

Allegro molto e vivace

Variations on "God Save the King"

Ludwig van Beethoven
1770–1827
WoO 78

Thema

Var. I

Var. II

Var. III

Var. VI
Allegro, alla marcia

Var. VII

tenuto

Coda

Symphony No. 2 in D Major

First Movement Excerpt

Ludwig van Beethoven
1770-1827
Op. 36
originally for orchestra

Symphony No. 2 in D Major

Third Movement Excerpt, "Scherzo"

Ludwig van Beethoven
1770-1827
Op. 36
originally for orchestra

Symphony No. 3 in E-flat Major
"Eroica"
First Movement Excerpt

Ludwig van Beethoven
1770-1827
Op. 55
originally for orchestra

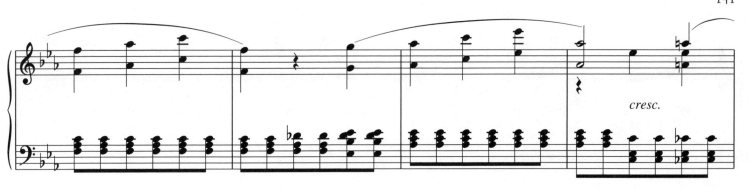

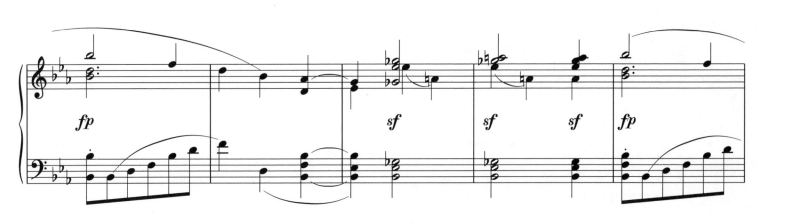

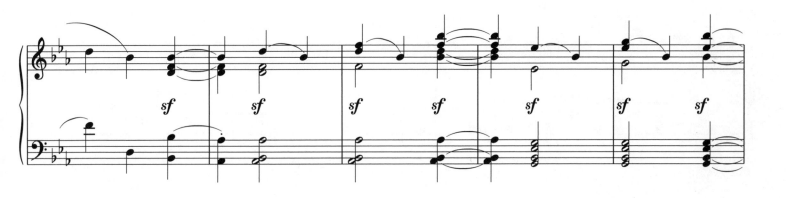

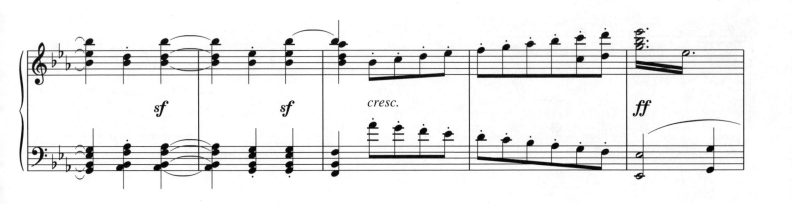

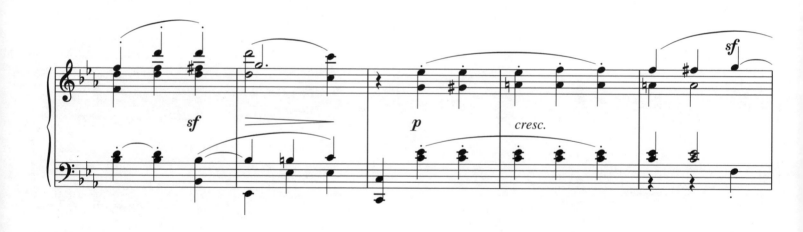

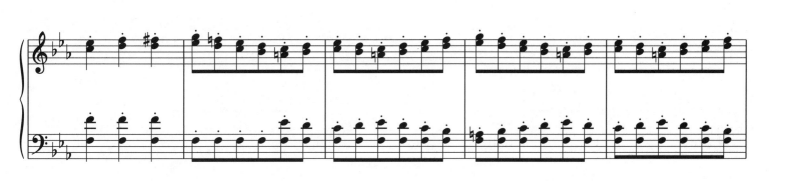

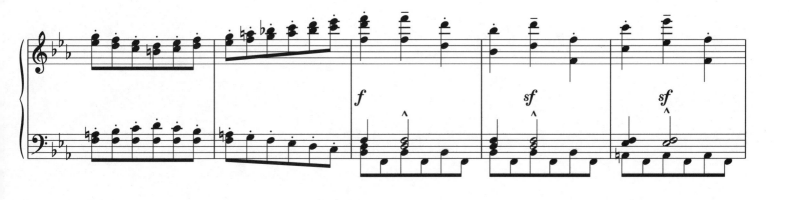

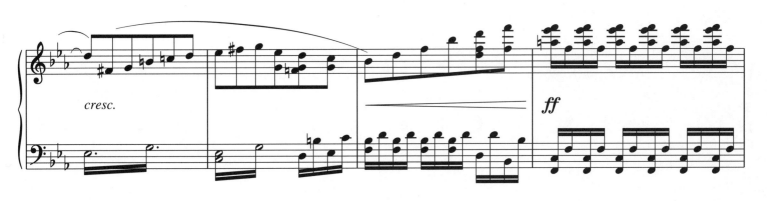

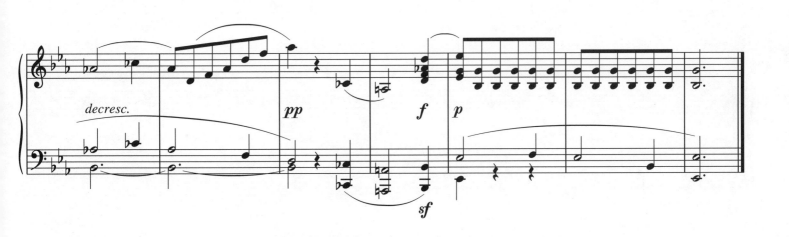

Symphony No. 4 in B-flat Major

First Movement Excerpt

Ludwig van Beethoven
1770-1827
Op. 60
originally for orchestra

Symphony No. 5 in C Minor
First Movement Excerpt

Ludwig van Beethoven
1770-1827
Op. 67
originally for orchestra

Symphony No. 5 in C Minor
Second Movement Excerpt

Ludwig van Beethoven
1770-1827
Op. 67
originally for orchestra

Andante con moto

Symphony No. 5 in C Minor
Third Movement Excerpt

Ludwig van Beethoven
1770-1827
Op. 67
originally for orchestra

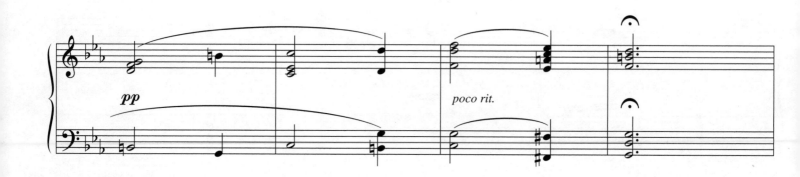

Symphony No. 5 in C Minor
Fourth Movement Excerpt

Ludwig van Beethoven
1770-1827
Op. 67
originally for orchestra

Symphony No. 6 in F Major
"Pastoral"
First Movement Excerpt, ("Awakening of cheerful feelings on arrival in the country")

Ludwig van Beethoven
1770-1827
Op. 68
originally for orchestra

Symphony No. 6 in F Major
"Pastoral"
Third Movement Excerpt, ("Merry gathering of the countryfolk")

Ludwig van Beethoven
1770-1827
Op. 68
originally for orchestra

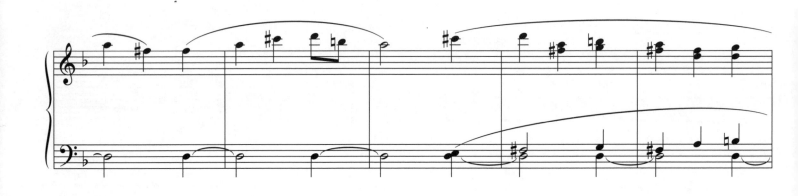

Symphony No. 6 in F Major
"Pastoral"
Fifth Movement Excerpt, ("Shepherd's song. Happy and grateful feelings after the storm")

Ludwig van Beethoven
1770-1827
Op. 68
originally for orchestra

Symphony No. 7 in A Major
First Movement Excerpt

Ludwig van Beethoven
1770-1827
Op. 92
originally for orchestra

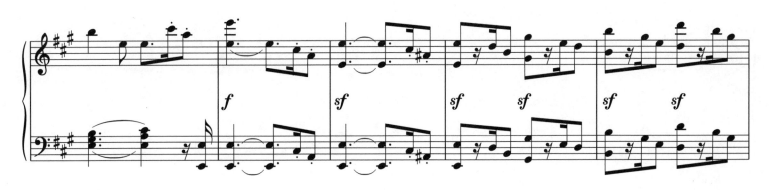

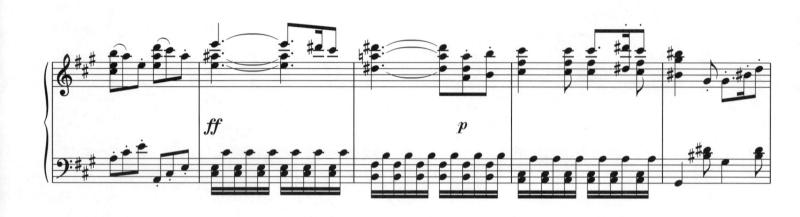

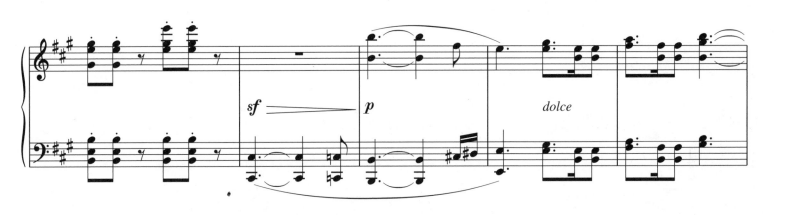

Symphony No. 7 in A Major
Second Movement Excerpt

Ludwig van Beethoven
1770-1827
Op. 92
originally for orchestra

Symphony No. 7 in A Major

Third Movement Excerpt

Ludwig van Beethoven
1770-1827
Op. 92
originally for orchestra

196

Assai meno presto

p dolce

Symphony No. 8 in F Major
First Movement Excerpt

Ludwig van Beethoven
1770-1827
Op. 93
originally for orchestra

Symphony No. 9 in D minor

Fourth Movement Excerpt
"Ode to Joy"

Ludwig van Beethoven
1770-1827
Op. 125
originally for orchestra

Violin Concerto in D Major

First Movement Excerpt

Ludwig van Beethoven
1770-1827
Op. 61
originally for violin and orchestra

Turkish March
from THE RUINS OF ATHENS

Ludwig van Beethoven
1770-1827
Op. 113

Wellington's Victory
Themes

Ludwig van Beethoven
1770-1827
Op. 91
originally for orchestra

Tempo di Marcia
"Rule Britannia"

Tempo di Marcia
"Marlborough"